19 IS A LA

C000126074

6 Steps To Financi.

Fulfilment As A Young Lady

MONICA ORANUGO ACHUGAMONYE

19 Is A Late Start

6 Steps to Financial Freedom and Fulfilment as a Young Lady

© **2020 Monica Oranugo Achugamonye**

DEDICATION

I dedicate this book first, to the Almighty God.

I also dedicate this book to my Dad, Vincent Oranugo. My mum, Francisca Oranugo of blessed memory. My sister, Patricia Oranugo Eke of blessed memory, and my siblings.

My parents brought me up in a good Christian, healthy, hardworking, humble, and happy home. This has helped me prevail through challenges as a young lady.

And to all the young ladies out there who are earnestly in search of success, I also dedicate this book to you.

TABLE OF CONTENTS

CHAPTER 1:

CAN I MAKE IT AS A YOUNG LADY IN A FOREIGN COUNTRY?

"Finding faith in the middle is the most challenging part of our walk to victory."

MY FIRST DAY IN EUROPE

I can still feel every bit of experience like it happened yesterday. It was about 3 pm when my father received a call from my sister, Ada. Ada told my father that she would love me to come and live with her in the Netherlands. I was in the living room with my Dad when the call came in. When she finished talking with my dad, he handed the phone to me and that was when my sister told me her plans. I had mixed feelings, as I was already very comfortable around my dad and friends, and the thought of relocating was a hard pill to swallow.

I recalled one evening, I went towards the balcony where my dad was seated and asked him, "Daddy, can I have a word with you?" He answered, "Sure, come sit beside me." I said, "Daddy, I appreciate the fact that 'sis' Ada wants to take me abroad, but I don't want to go."

My dad wanted to know why I didn't want to go, and I made him understand that I needed to be beside him to assist him with his daily errands, given that mum had passed away not long before that incident. My dad smiled, and while holding me tight in his arms, he said, "Nwabugo (a name my parents called me), my daughter. I have lived my life, and now, you have to live yours." He cautioned that I had to seize the opportunity to build a better and valuable life for myself.

He continued by asking me a question, "Nwabugo, my daughter, I admire the fact that you want to stay with me, but have you forgotten that you just finished secondary school, and will have to go to the university?" He continued, "When you enrol in the university, will you leave school every day to take care of me?" I answered, "No." He then concluded, "My daughter, meet your sister in the Netherlands. She needs you more than I do, and be a good girl when you get there."

It was almost time for me to leave, and my Dad organized a family party for me, and it was outstanding. The night of the party was emotional for me. After the event, he called me again, and gave me a lot of advice. He also gave me his rosary, saying, "Know that it has been the Lord that has been on our side and has brought us this far. Don't forget all that your mum and I taught you." It was emotional hearing these words from my dad, and I wished I could just stay back in Nigeria, but I knew leaving was for my own good. From the moment I set my mind to travel abroad, I could already see myself living the Hollywood dream.

In a nutshell, after I received the call and set my mind to travel, the excitement set in. Many thoughts followed. I could envisage myself arriving at the airport in this marvellous country. I could see how my life will turn around faster than I could imagine. I could immediately feel that I was ascending to a different level in life. With these feelings settling in, and with no real-life experience, I quickly made up my mind to transform the lives of my family immediately I got to Europe. I began to imagine how I would build them another house in less than no time, and get them a car and a driver.

My imaginations were running wild as I could see myself promising my friends to help them become better immediately I got to Europe, and start making money. I could imagine a perfect life with no challenges and was confident that every imagination of mine would soon become a reality.

Living in a foreign country as a young lady can be challenging. It comes with different life experiences, and most often, it comes with the feeling of excitement and high expectations. However, when reality sets in, it brings so much discouragement and surprises to the extent that if not well handled, could ruin a lifetime dream. My intention for you is not to let you focus on the negative aspects of the journey, but first, to bring you to the realization that it is possible to handle these challenges, and that life could be different and exciting if we are well prepared to face reality.

Often, most of the people that travel abroad get trapped in a false reality that life is a 'bed of roses.' However, when they eventually hit reality, they become overwhelmed with the sudden discrepancy between their expectations and reality. Most people even feel like giving up when reality hits them.

Yes, I know exactly how these experiences and the feelings it brings can beat you to the ground. I have been through some of these bitter experiences, and I understand what it means. The feeling of leaving your home country, families, friends, culture, food, and more is a big decision to deal with. Not to talk of the cultural shocks that accompany these drastic changes.

The journey starts with 'short-lived' courage, aspirations, ambitions, and hope for a better life, the zeal for a better future, and the quest for opportunities. These have caused many to travel thousands of miles away from home to find new homes and opportunities, hoping they can achieve better education, better financial outcomes, good health, among others. However, the challenges that come with this venture can seem like a roller coaster ride.

THE EXCITEMENT CURVE

The entire process starts with excitement. The joy of achieving this expected breakthrough is often the first thing to deal with when a young lady travels abroad. The momentum is often very high at the beginning. The expectations are most often very high.

The excitement triggers friends, and family members to go beyond their reach to support the cause, both emotionally and financially, with the hope of reaping the benefits within a short time.

The excitement of traveling abroad, the esteem it brings, and the quest for "greener pastures" has made some families go to the extent of selling their own homes to sponsor their relatives abroad. The sacrifices made by both the 'adventurer' and concerned family members most often sets the bar of expectation so high, that 'the traveller' suddenly begins to think that traveling abroad is equal to success.

However, as soon as they settle at their destination, the reality sets in. 'The excitement and high expectations,' meet reality. Sometimes, it feels like the harder they push, nothing seems to work, and this may leave the person with depression and total confusion.

The reality sets in when you face real-life situations, like not only feeling like you are a stranger in another land, but also understanding that everything you expected to achieve so easily wasn't as easy as you thought. At this point, the excitement curve falls. This often starts with discouragement, and sometimes, you might even feel like packing your luggage and returning home. And then, a reality check sets in again, and you begin to ask yourself: "What about the sacrifice of my parents? What will my friends say if I return home without meeting my promises to them? What about my commitments to give my family members a better life?" You might become trapped in a world of your own, and you might even see life pushing you to the edge, a very uncomfortable place for anyone to be in, especially in a foreign country.

It is a sad situation that many people get caught up in this phase, and struggle for a very long time with no way out. It is tempting to think things were meant to be that way, a situation many young ladies can relate to. This has also pushed many young ladies to be trapped in habits, and situations they didn't bargain for, or see coming.

However, I want you to imagine how different your life could be today if you could find a way out of your current situation. How you could transition from that low-paying job, to a job that can bring all of those imaginations to reality. I want you to imagine what life will be if you stop hiding and thinking you are a disgrace to your family. I want you to imagine how life could be if you stop showing up strong in public, and crying aloud in your closet. I want you to imagine crushing your academic goals without a limitation, even after what many wasted years.

These are possible, and it starts with you taking the first step to financial freedom and fulfilment, which we will talk about soon. Before we do that, let's share more about some challenges that accompanies being a young lady in a foreign land.

DEALING WITH CULTURAL SHOCKS

Imagine the excitement that you are traveling to the land of 'milk and honey,' just to realise that immediately you arrived, you find everyone speaking a strange language. The first thought comes into your mind, and I hear you saying to yourself "Wait a minute, how will I be able to achieve success in this land without being able to understand the language." This is the same thinking I had when I landed in Paris 17 years ago. My first shock was the language. I couldn't understand a single word in French. I was confused and anxious about what will happen to me if I missed my connecting flight to Amsterdam. However, I magically navigated through the entire process without missing my flight. Today, I still can't figure out how I got through the process of connecting to my next flight, but the fact that I am writing to you now is a sign that I made it through. I want you to pause a minute, and visualise yourself in that same scenario. They are two options you have at hand. The first is that "I don't understand the French language and therefore, I can't catch my connection flight," and the second option is that "I don't know how I will make it, but I need to do it anyway, because I can't afford to miss my flight." Just this way of thinking changes everything about being stuck in any situation.

However, they are also many thoughts that came to my mind while I was trying to find my way to my connecting flight; "I wish I took my French lessons seriously while I was in college," "If I knew that I will go through all of this, I wouldn't have accepted to embark on the trip. "Life has a way of throwing us back each time we are about to cross to another level". Imagine what would have become of me if I had given up at that moment. Going back to Nigeria would have been more expensive than continuing from Paris to Amsterdam. That is exactly what happens to us when we give up, or when we refuse to take an action when we have to. Imagine how your life could be different today if you decide that no matter what you go through, you will overcome. I am not saying it is easy, but it is simple and doable. We just need a guide, and some encouragement.

The fact that you need to learn an unfamiliar language to fit into an unfamiliar environment can be a major challenge. I remember my first week in

Amsterdam. I was afraid of learning an unfamiliar language all over again. I could not understand a single word from the Dutch language, which was the principal language of communication. I couldn't even express myself in the least and common word like "Goede morgen". This brought the fear of even attempting to learn anything or go anywhere, even to the shop. Other dimensions of the challenges also came in the aspect of food. I remember how difficult it was for me to fit into the new food culture. The food tasted strange. The African food I was used to was very expensive to afford. In my first month abroad, I developed poor eating habits, lost my appetite and developed stomach upset several times. The psychological effect of not having the same food as I used to have back in Nigeria all set in. This made life more overwhelming. Notwithstanding, I came to the realisation that all of this was happening for my good. God has a way of taking us through the storm in a way that when it is over, we know exactly how to handle bigger storms when we come across them. That was exactly what was happening. You might go through the financial storms now, you might go through educational storms now, or storms, but I just want you to know that it is possible to prevail and emerge victorious.

Before moving ahead, let's reflect on this scenario. Allow me take you to a country like Nigeria, where there are over 200 local languages. It is very usual that many people hardly speak over two languages out of over 200 of these languages. When this thought came into my mind, I could feel my mind being challenged and I started asking myself, "If I could not learn over one language in my native land, what more of a different and unfamiliar land all together." All this then brought the thought of missing home, which had now become a faraway country, because there was no turning back. The high expectations from family members, friends, acquaintances, and religious bodies were still all in my imagination. I kept asking myself, how many years will it take me to integrate, learn the people, their culture, the language, the way of life, and the work environment. To make things more completed, I started worrying about how hard it would be for me to get a residence permit. Thinking about getting an excellent education might then become a thing of the future. Despite these, I want to assure you that all these questions and worries that might go through your head and mind are very normal. I will explain more about this later.

Thinking Education

One of the biggest challenges I had to deal with was deciding whether to pursue education, money, or learn the Dutch language. It was a hard choice, because all of them were equally very important. I kept thinking, "If I can't understand the language, how on earth would I even think about studying in that language?" I could literally see three years becoming so many years of no results. It is kind of interesting how our mind can play with us and shut us down. This was me, making no effort or taking any action, already telling myself it was not possible to achieve success. These are all false realities that happens in our minds all the time. I guess the question you would like to ask me is how did I overcome the mediocrity and emerge victorious today. I will share the step-by-step process with you in the subsequent chapters.

Is It Possible to Make it as a Young Lady in a Foreign Country?

You might ask yourself if it is possible to grow beyond your present circumstances. How long would it take me to overcome? What are the steps I need to take in other to achieve success? The pressure and high expectations from the people looking up to you even makes the situation worse, most of the time. It makes it seem like life has placed you in the middle of the sea, with a very heavy storm going on. It may even feel like there is no hope for tomorrow. Notwithstanding, one reason I wrote this book is because I understand that in the middle of every storm, there is the Invisible One who has the power to stop the storm. All you need to do is cry for help, and the solution will appear. Imagine what would have happened to me if I did not walk out of my fears, with the help of the prominent people around me. I would not have had the privilege to tell you my story at this point in time. For every pain you go through, there is light at the end of the tunnel. All you need to do to get to the light is to follow the rays of the light. This book, "19 is a late start" has been written from my heart, not only to share a victor's story, but to walk with you in your own journey to victory.

CHAPTER 2:

THE TRICK TO OVERCOMING THE FEAR OF FAILURE AS A YOUNG LADY

"A clear strategy is the most powerful GPS to success."

THE FIRST STEPS MATTER A LOT

I n life, the people you meet can either add value to your life, or take value out of your life. Have you been around a certain group of people who will unapologetically tell you it is not possible to make it in life without suffering? Or, tell you that the way they know is the only way to success? Many people sacrifice a lot before travelling abroad, sometimes large financial debts are even incurred prior to travelling. This experience often pushes them to think that making money is the priority immediately they arrive abroad. Well, they are close to the truth. This was also my thinking immediately I arrived abroad. I thought it was time to go out to make money through all means possible. This is the point where the people you meet, or have access to have a key role to play in your life.

I remember when I first arrived Netherlands, and my sister, Ada, told me I will have to enrol in a language school. She explained the importance to me. This was not really my plan or expectation, but I am glad I had such a person to give me this priceless advice. This piece of advice was the GPS I needed to get to the destination I find myself today. I had to put my best in it, because I was very clear on learning the Dutch language. I knew it was the basic key to unlocking future doors. As a young lady who moved to a foreign country at 19, I was asking myself lots of questions. One of my top questions was how possible it would be for me to learn a language I have never come across before, and understand it. Notwithstanding, the moment I took the step of faith to start the journey, without knowing what the outcome would be, I encountered success. I am aware you might ask the same question. I want you to know that I understand all the questions you are asking, and all the challenges you are going through. Although my challenges and yours might not be exactly the same, I want you to know that the first solution to a challenge is taking a step of faith in a direction of success. The same way I took the step of faith and started learning Dutch, having no clue if I will ever understand, is the same step of faith I want you to take now to get out of any challenge that might keep you in one spot. I know you might say that I was just 19, and I had enough time to experiment. However, that is not the case. If I had waited for this long to take an action, my 19 years will start counting from today. So, no matter how old you might be, if you are not yet meeting your desired results, I want you to visit "my 19"; that moment when I wished I could have worked to make some money, but had to endure language lessons. The good news is that, it is possible these days to study, and work, no matter how busy your schedule might be. I really understand how you feel, your worries, your fears, your imaginations, anticipations, discouragement, doubts. I passed through it, and with the help of God, and the lovely people I came across, I am glad I made it, and I know you will definitely make it.

I remember the 13th day of September 2003, when I first arrived at the airport, Schiphol Amsterdam, in the Netherlands. On my way to the exit door, an immigration officer approached me and said something in a language I did not understand. I think he started speaking in Dutch, and then later switched to English. What I remember well was that it took me a while to find myself, and ask him to repeat what he was saying for me to understand what he wanted. Although he started communicating to me in English, it took me a while to process every word and sentence before giving the right answer. This is just to let you know that even in an English-speaking country, you could still experience the language barrier. A lot of foreigners living in English-speaking countries can testify that, even though they can communicate well in English, the cultural and psychological barriers are still obvious. This means that your ability to succeed is beyond just understanding a language, as we will discover subsequently.

One thing that also baffled me, and made me discouraged was the kind of buildings and structures I saw from the airport to my sister's house. The picture I had about Europe was a beautiful and heavenly place with gorgeous structures. The Hollywood movies I had watched informed my picture of Europe. Another big issue to deal with was that when I arrived my sister's house, her children were speaking and asking me so many questions in Dutch, a language that was already giving me a phobia. This made things even more complex. It was frustrating. I was at that point where I was happy seeing my family, but I was not happy because of the context of things at that moment.

OVERCOMING FEAR

It was time to enrol for the Dutch lesson, and that rekindled all my fears. All the memories of the airport encounter with the immigration officer, and my encounter with my sister's kids came rushing back. My expectation was to enrol directly into the university, and not start another language lesson again. I thought about all my friends back in Nigeria who were all gaining admission into the university. I missed home, to the extent that I was crying, and I even told my sister I wanted to return to Nigeria. Things grew worse when I learned that I also had to take my nursing school lessons in the Dutch language. I missed life in my beautiful hometown. I was born and brought up in a noble city called Warri, in Delta state which is located in the southern part of Nigeria.

This part of Nigeria is very fun to live in. Like they say, "Warri no dey carry last". A phrase I loved so much, which was used to describe the Waferians (the Warri people). This means that people from this part of Nigeria never bow to defeat, but here I was, fully defeated by a mere language. What was running through my mind was the fact that, if I could not learn an additional language back in my country with hundreds of different local languages, how on earth would I be able to learn the Dutch Language?

At this point, I was more focused on my family, and friends; how far they would have gone with their studies within the year I would spend learning Dutch. I had a lot going on in my mind. I was asking too many questions at a time. I felt lost, and thought it would not be possible for me to learn the language and understand it. Notwithstanding, I gradually started accepting the fact that there was nothing I could change about the situation I was facing, rather, I would have to accept it and deal with it.

WHAT MADE THE DIFFERENCE?

My first breakthrough in the language struggle came forth on this fateful day. I was the youngest in the midst of married men and women, mothers and fathers. I was the only young lady in my class. My performance in class was very poor. This class was to prepare those who wanted to learn Dutch as a basic tool to help them find a job, but here I was. I wanted to learn it for college application, and yet, I was the student with the worst performance in class. However, although my performance was very poor, I didn't give up. I had a conviction in my heart that things will be better one day. As faith has a way to get us around our belief, something happened that turned things around for my good. There was this Godsent man in my class. His name was Erasmus, a Nigerian too. We usually called him Raz man, which is actually the short form of raster man. He loved reggae music, and loved to attend summer reggae festivals. He noticed I was not doing well in class and he called me one day to encourage me to put more interest in the language. He emphasized that the lesson will help me in life, and it is the starting point to having a successful career. He advised me and challenged me to make sure I become the best student in class by the next class assignment. It was a wakeup call for me. I had someone to hold me accountable. In class, he was like a father to me. He helped monitor my performance. At first, I did not like the idea, but when I sat and thought of it, I found reasons to take his advice seriously. This did not mean that my sister did not explain or encourage me on the importance of these lessons. She did her best, but I think a couple of things were missing, the accountability part of the advice.

The follow-up of Raz man made the difference, and pushed me to attain the success I wanted. I found the strength in accountability and I exploited it to attain a different height of success in life. Let us look at it from two dimensions. Although my sister explained the importance of studying Dutch to me, I was missing the daily encouragement needed for success. The ability to succeed is beyond just knowing what to do to succeed. Success is more about the daily mindset. Constant accountability drives success in life. Raz man did not really do much per se in teaching me Dutch, but he gave me something missing in my life. Immediately, I accepted to follow his advice and to report to him daily on my progress. I developed new strategies to overcome my fears. I would share some of my fears with him, and he would give me some words of wisdom necessary for my success. Since I noticed that continuous accountability was the key to success, I have been able to leverage this technique, not only to succeed in life but to help others do the same.

When I was ready to share one of my biggest strengths to succeed with people who might go through similar mental challenges, I had to replicate the strength I found in working with Raz man to get this message to you. I was sure of what I wanted to do, and how I wanted to do it. However, I was also conscious of the fact that with my busy schedule as a nurse practitioner, it might not be easy for me to be disciplined and meet my goals. I got myself a coach, and in less than no time, we put up a strategy. We completed the strategy, and the result is the book you are reading. They are two sides of the equation here. I could still do this without the help of my coach, but I know that it would have taken me an eternity to finish. It would also have remained in my computer for maybe another three years, before getting out for public consumption, that's if it ever made its way out to the public. With the help of my coach, we got this done in less than no time. It went faster than I could ever imagine. That is the same thing I want for you. I have been under the mentorship of coaches that improved my life, and made my journey to success smoother. One reason I also wrote this book is to educate young ladies on the importance of having an accountability system, that will help them navigate effortlessly through their success journey.

When I finally finished my Dutch lesson, I enrolled in the International Business Management (IBMS). They taught the program in English, and I was happy because I thought I finally found what I needed. To my surprise, I could not understand the course, although it was taught in English. I was struggling with it. You can imagine that despite the fact that I understood English language well, it was stressful for me studying IBMS in English language. This is just to let you know that often, the problem is just constructed in our minds, and might be different when we face them in real life. English language could also be a barrier, especially when the pursuit does not align with your purpose.

Rev. Fr. Chima also enhanced my success journey. During my days in the Dutch class, I went to him after service in church, complaining about how stressful my study with the IBMS program was, and also to explain to him that my interest was in nursing. He was an angel God sent to me. He encouraged me, and gave me reasons why I should follow what my heart was after. He introduced me to a lady who could give me more information about the nursing program in Dutch. After meeting with this lady, I was so encouraged. She made me see the possibilities in the midst of impossibilities. I returned home, and told my sister I did not want to continue with the IBMS program, and that I wanted to study nursing. She was happy with my decision, and her husband helped me find a nursing school in Belgium. It was not an easy journey, but the joy of knowing that I was pursuing my dream program kept me going.

BLENDING WANTS AND NEEDS

Working while studying is one of the major challenges to success. This is because it is psychologically draining, and it impairs your ability to succeed, if it is not well managed. Effective accountability can enhance your ability to successfully manage work and study. I found out later that I struggled throughout my nursing school because I did not have people like Raz man that could be the GPS to my success. However, I also learned that I did not give up, because I was passionate about what I was doing. You must realise that there are two main important aspects here that could facilitate your success rate. The first is getting an accountability coach, and the second is going after your passion. However, it is also clear that a lot of us do not know if we are living our purpose or not. This is where the power of a coach overcomes the mere drive of passion. Although I knew there was something great in me that the world needed to experience, I was not too sure what exactly it was, or how I could get it out to the world, until I came across my coach. In less than one hour of discussion, I found extra strength, and hope that lightened me up and opened me to my full potential.

After completing my language and nursing studies, I learned a couple of lessons. When I overcame my first challenge, which was the language barrier, it encouraged me to see that it will be possible to achieve other goals. This understanding was very useful for me when I finished school, and started working. I noticed that when I started working and interacting more with people, my speaking and understanding of the language was constantly being improved. This also teaches us that success is a work in progress, and not a momentary achievement. The more you use what you have, the better you become in that aspect. Today, I am proud to say I feel valuable when I am in my uniform as a nurse practitioner in one of the most prestigious medical institutions in the world. I am proud of the look of respect on people's faces, with an expression that screams, "Who is this young coloured lady with the ambulance team?" every time I am on duty. I also remembered that during my first internship in a home care centre, I met an old lady whom has never had a coloured lady help her out. She was furious and refused my help, but the nurse in charge said it was either we both took care of her, or we both leave, and she will not be provided care that morning. She later accepted that I make her bed. Out of curiosity, she asked me, "Which country are you from?" I told her I was from Nigeria. She asked me how far my country was from

Belgium, and I answered her. She paused and said, "So, you came all the way from your home town to help and take care of us?" I said, "Yes, I did."

Situations like this are daily life challenges, living and working as a young lady in a foreign country. However, they should act as a tool of encouragement, rather than a tool for discouragement. It's more rewarding if we could ignore, and not pay too much attention to them, and keep focusing on the vision and goals ahead of us. A spirit that never gives up is a winning spirit.

I quite remember that they were two other African students who started the same nursing course like me, and both of them all gave up during their internship for one reason or the other. The reason I share this with you is that, I realised one of the most common reason for quitting is a lack of clarity, hope, self-confidence and faith. I have come to the realisation that these things can be achieved effortlessly with the help of someone that understands the challenges and has been part of it. My struggle through school, and coming out strong was not a simple task. As a young lady in school, I found it difficult to interact with other students because of the language barrier. Most of the things others see as normal, was abnormal or not accepted in my culture. For example, you will hear a 19-year-old girl saying her mum still helps her with her laundry, her cooking and even irons her clothes, just to name a few. This is the complete opposite where I come from. At my young age, I learnt life the hard way and how to be independent and successful. Initially, it was not easy, but as time went on, I began to gain strength.

My work experience after school was also another phase of the challenge. I had to work harder daily to prove that I am competent enough to work at the emergency department.

These phases of learning have made me strong. My goal is that you realise that, no matter what you might go through, you can also find strength. Let's win together.

CHAPTER 3:

---

19 IS A LATE START

"No matter what time you start, you have equal chances to success as someone that started a couple of years before you."

HOLDING SPACE FOR SUCCESS

L et's start by clearing the air, and holding space for everyone to succeed. You must have come across the saying that the journey to success is not lonely. No matter what time you start, you have equal chances to succeed as someone that started a couple of years before you. Also, you even have greater chances to succeed more than them because you leverage the lessons from their journey to optimize yours. A late start does not mean you cannot succeed. A late start comes to raise the awareness that you would have been better off if you had done certain things earlier in life. However, it is also not an opportunity for you to play the blame game, because blaming yourself will lead you nowhere. The only key to success is to come to the understanding that you are worth more than your present value, as my coach will always say. The moment you understand that you can do more, you immediately see the possibility of doing more. The only reason we have people staying on the same spot for a very long time is that they have accepted the 'status quo', or have talked themselves into thinking that they are not better than their current situation.

Achieving financial freedom and fulfilment as a young lady is one of the biggest milestones in the journey to success. However, let us get some clarity on what we mean by financial freedom. You do not need to be a millionaire to attain financial freedom. In simpler terms, we can say that you have come to a stage in your life where you do not need to depend on anyone else to live a happy lifestyle. I am also very aware that lifestyle differs from individuals, and what we might consider success for one party, might not be the same for the next party. This also brings us to talk about the phrase "understanding your purpose in life." As young ladies, we all have dreams, whether big or small. Whether these dreams align with your purpose in life is another question. Why is the concept of fulfilment fundamental? You could have financial freedom and remain unfulfilled, because they have not met your God-given purpose in life. As a young lady, what gives you direction in life is both the pursuit of financial freedom and fulfilment. I will say that fulfilment is like the destination of your dream vacation, and financial freedom is the means to get there. With the understanding of this concept, you will agree with me you might have enough money to pay for a dream vacation, but if you do not have access (visa) to the location of your dream vacation, then you will not be fulfilled because you have not achieved your desires.

In summary, fulfilment is achieving the desire of your heart. This might be to attain a certain level of education, get married, have a cheerful home, and become an inspiration to many and more. These are the things that money cannot buy. We must build them into your journey of success. Financial freedom comes in to facilitate the process of you achieving your fulfilment as a young lady.

At this point, I will like you to take a moment and reflect on your values as a young lady.

- What is stopping you from achieving the life you want?

- What is stopping you from having a well-paid job?
- What is stopping you from writing that book?
- What is stopping you from starting that business?
- What is stopping you from getting married?
- What is stopping you from having a peaceful home?

These are all questions that, if not carefully answered, will slow you from achieving financial freedom and fulfilment in life. However, the good news is that you are reading this book now. In this book, I have been able to put in place the same strategies that have helped me and the others I have mentored attain financial freedom and fulfilment. In six simple steps, I will share the strategies/processes that make an enormous difference in my life and other people's lives. I want you to be part of it. These steps include:

STEP I: OVERCOMING DISCOURAGEMENT, AND SELF-DOUBT

Most of the time, the reason it takes too long to get to a solution is not really because the answer is difficult, but because we over-complicate the solution. Thus, the solution becomes more of a mystery than a means to solve the problem. This brings in discouragement and self-doubt, which are the roots of failure. One of the first steps to success is your ability to fight discouragement and self-doubt. The way the society and our community are designed can sometimes unconsciously promote, discourage, and make us feel that because everyone is doing the same thing, we should also follow suit. In this step, as you will read later in chapter four of this book, I share with you how I faced discouragement, and how I converted that into winning stories, rather than letting the situation kick me back in life.

STEP II: UNDERSTANDING THE DIFFERENCE BETWEEN MONEY AND SUCCESS

The pursuit of money can make you go the wrong way sometimes. Many big dreams die, not because the people having those dreams could not achieve them, but because they fail to understand the difference between money and success. More than 90% of Africans who travel abroad always have high expectations and hopes, and they expect sudden financial breakthrough upon their arrival. However, when they finally arrive, there is the sudden realization that dreams can only become a reality with massive action involved. Money can come without success, but success never comes without money. In this step, I help my young ladies understand the strategies they could adopt to avoid being distracted by the pursuit of money in their journey to financial freedom and fulfilment. Money can even be a stumbling block to real success if it is misunderstood as success.

STEP III: EDUCATION IS PART OF YOUR SUCCESS

Every individual on earth is different. You have to be able to identify your unique strength in life. This will help you to understand what works for you. Many people have gone astray in life today because they think they can do the same thing that others do, and succeed the way they succeeded. I understood from the onset of my career that achieving a better education was a plus for me to achieve success in life. In this step, I share with young ladies, the techniques I used to advance in my academic studies despite all odds.

STEP IV: DEALING WITH DAILY CHALLENGES

In life, every single day comes with its challenges. How we choose to accept consciously, handle, and go about the daily difficulties matter a lot. Social, relationship, and emotional challenges in life could be well-managed and converted to stepping stones. On the other hand, when these challenges are mismanaged, it could cause delays, distractions, stress, frustration, and even health challenges. In these steps, I shared with young ladies, some of my winning strategies in handling daily challenges and how they could draw inspiration from them to attract the success they seek in life.

STEP V: DISCIPLINE, LIFESTYLE, AND HABITS

Discipline will be one of your biggest tools if you're going to succeed in whatsoever you do. Your ability to start and finish any task without distraction is determined by how disciplined you are. In this step, we talk about two types of discipline in the journey of success and in the life of a young lady. This could also apply to young men, but the reason I am particular about young ladies is because I am sharing my experiences as a young lady. I have a special attraction to seeing young ladies become successful in life. In this step, I also shared the importance of a healthy lifestyle and healthy habits in the journey of success.

STEP VI: PERSISTENCE

Persistence, what a sweet word to pronounce, but not too easy to keep up with. It takes God's grace, courage, sound mind, focus, and good advice to keep persisting to the end of your goal. One of the biggest lessons I have learnt during my success journey is that persistence comes with relentless action. I also understand that the reward at the end of the road needs to be greater than the pain. How can you make this happen so you can prevail at the end of the road? In this step, I use my own experiences and winning strategies to guide you on what exactly you can do to stay persistent and successful.

CHAPTER 4:

◆— • ——◆

OVERCOMING DISCOURAGEMENT AND SELF-DOUBT

"Discouragement and self-doubt do not don't definitely imply you are defeated".

STRIVING IN A CHALLENGING ENVIRONMENT AS A YOUNG LADY

L iving as a young lady in a new environment can be challenging. Adapting to an environment and learning new cultural values is also time consuming. Learning a new language, a new way of living, new belief systems, adjusting to new weather conditions, and many more might seem impossible from the first point of view. This might also set in discouragement and self-doubt. It can even go to the extent that you will begin to lose interest in the things you used to like. This may include, but not limited to, fatigue, inferiority complex and depression. Despite all these feelings, things could still be hopeful. Your strength in times of difficulties is not defined by what happens to you, but by how you handle what happens to you. When you feel this way sometimes, I want you to understand that the feeling is normal. Even the most successful people still go through discouragement and self-doubt. The difference is how they handle the situations.

OVERCOMING DISCOURAGEMENT, AND SELF-DOUBT

Discouragement and self-doubt are parts of the process to success. It is not something you can completely escape from. So, what do you do with something that you cannot escape from? You find a way to handle it, right? Discouragement and self-doubt are handled in your daily engagements. You need to be able to train your system and routine in a way that automatically, and unconsciously fights discouragement. Discouragement does not mean that you are dumb or unintelligent. It should be a stepping stone to achieving your goals if you handle them well.

If only you could hold on, and not give in to discouragement's external and internal impulses, you will see that you can attain any height you want in life. You can become who you want to be, add value to your life, and others, only if you can handle discouragement. You will agree with me that you will become the source of strength for others whenever you can go through any challenging moment in life.

I was once there, and I know how it feels to be discouraged and how to overcome discouragement and self- doubt. I will take you through a few experiences I had while dealing with discouragement and self-doubt. I could have given up in these moments, but I stood firm and was able to have some encounters that turned things around for me. I remember there were periods during my school days that I felt like giving up. There were moments where struggled to pass my courses. I would sit in the same classroom with other students, and be taught by the same tutor, but I could not understand why I could not perform as great as other students. This was something I was not used to experiencing. I could blame it on the fact that I was studying in a foreign language. However, instead of laying blame, I had to find a way to prevail through the challenge. In my first year in nursing school, I failed all courses. The only course I passed was hospital practical training. This was the very first time in life I had this kind of 'huge failure.' I was frustrated, unhappy, and I lost appetite for food to the extent that I developed ulcers. This led to continuous headaches, sleepless nights, and stress. The workload from school was not helping the situation at all. At this point, discouragement set in. I began to doubt myself. I started asking myself questions that were not really helping the situation. I started talking down to myself, saying things like, "I can't do this." I was thinking of giving up and maybe just turn to an easier path of life, like getting married to someone already successful, so that I do not have to do more. I also thought of dropping out of school and just focus on picking up a basic job like I saw the other young ladies doing. I know that you might be going through some of these things right now or you know someone that is currently going through them. My advice at this point is that quitting is more strenuous than continuing. You can only discover and appreciate this advice after you prevail through any situation.

The period I was going through all the above challenges as a young lady was one of the most critical periods in my life. That was a point in my life where I had to define if I would be successful in surrendering to the challenges of society. It was a moment I had to rethink my life, and what I wanted out of it. When I thought about quitting sometimes, I remembered the encouraging words my dad spoke to me before I travelled abroad. I also remember the joy that was on the faces of the people who celebrated with me when I was about to travel. I thought about all my friends back home that have gone ahead of me in education. I had to find almost anything that could encourage me to finish successfully. Finding encouragement in the things that matter in my life, rather than looking at what was not working was one of my major strengths. This is a major strategy that helped me to prevail and complete my nursing school. It is a straightforward strategy to fight discouragement, and I love it because everyone can apply it to succeed. When you are discouraged and feeling like nothing is working, I want you to focus your attention on the benefits of finishing what you are doing, rather than thinking about how challenging it might be to go through with it. This fundamental shift in thinking will make a significant difference in your life, and move you to your next level of success.

You must have read earlier in the text that even successful people need to deal with discouragement and self-doubt. I want to bring it to a more practical level. You will agree with me that there are some days when you just don't feel like getting out of bed or going to work, even when you know that that is the right thing to do. Just imagine if you allow a discouraging mindset to take over at that particular moment. You will definitely lose that job if you don't go to work. No work or activity will take place if you do not get out of bed. You won't even be able to have breakfast if you don't get out of bed, except you have someone else bring it to you. You will also agree that it is more expensive to have someone else bring it to you, compared to going out to purchase it for yourself. Imagine the amount of money you could save if you decide to make breakfast for yourself, instead of ordering it from an app on your phone, and having it delivered to you in bed. In the same line, giving up on your dream is just like you deciding to stay in bed in the morning, and then ordering food from your mobile app. Life becomes more expensive for us if we refuse to fight discouragement. You have to get out of bed intentionally, even if you don't feel like to do that. You have to go to work, even if you don't feel like going. In the same way you reap the benefits of going to work when you don't feel like, is the same way you reap the benefits of life when you fight discouragement.

DISCOURAGEMENT IS A WINNING STRATEGY

When I understood how discouragement works and what I could do to stay motivated, it became one of my winning strategies continuously. After I graduated as a registered nurse, I saw the need to go extra miles in my educational career. I understood that I had to build a support system around me to fight discouragement and self-doubt. I also knew that there was nothing I could do successfully without the help of God Almighty. Also, the fact that I have been through some difficult moments and overcame them gave me more courage to pursue further success. With this mindset, I said to myself, "Girl, you did it before. So, you can do it again. Why not go for a master's degree?" However, just when I could gather enough courage to take the step of faith, self-doubt and comfort set in. I already had a part-time job with DD-Medicals, a family ambulance company in Turnhout, a city located in Belgium.

I had a good rapport with my boss, whose name was Danny, and he understood some of my worries because I had narrated my story and academic journey to him. He encouraged me enormously by sharing some of his son's experiences, who also had difficulties during his studies at the same nursing school I attended. He said, "My son, who is a native Dutch speaker, had challenges during school days. He spent five years in school. instead of three years, but he did not let the challenges overcome him. He was able to further his education and obtained a specialization certificate as an Emergency and Intensive Care Nurse." He was by then working in the emergency department of a medical unit. He said, "If he could do it, then, you can do it as well." This encouraged me a lot, and I applied for my specialization course in Intensive care and emergency. In the same way, you are going to meet great people along your way like Danny that will encourage you to take the next giant step in your life.

After the great encouragement from Danny, I did not allow discouragement and self-doubt to cloud my mind and take over me again. There have been occasions where my teachers told me, "Monica, maybe you should think of quitting these studies and go to the diploma nursing instead of continuing with the bachelor of science in nursing." They reminded me that the bachelor of science was too difficult for me. There were times when people that knew when I was studying would meet me on my way to or back from school and say to me, "*This your school sef, e no dey finish*?" – This is a common phrase in Nigeria that means "For how long will you keep doing this with no results?"

There are times when you might feel you have succeeded, but situations might come unexpectedly, and even those who believed in you might even doubt your capability. I had one of such experiences during one of my training sessions in an intensive care department. During this period, it seemed like all things went wrong. The nurses working with me in the same team were not supportive and encouraging at all. During my training evaluation, I got a negative review to the extent that the head of the nursing department of the intensive unit said to me vividly, "Monica, I do not see you being able to work or become an intensive care nurse. I suggest you should stop and just continue as a registered nurse. You cannot work in the ICU." After this incident, I was down and sick. I cried as if my whole world had come to an end. At this point, I started pondering on her idea. I started saying to myself, "I think she is right; I cannot do this." I immediately gave room for negative forces and thoughts when I started letting my thoughts dwell on ideas. My key advice is that anything you dislike, do not let your thought dwell on it.

WHY LEARN A LANGUAGE AGAINST ALL ODDS?

Initially, I did not know that learning the language

properly would facilitate my academic pursuit and life in general. Learning the Dutch language helped me to relate well with my community and attract the things I needed for success. A lot of native speaking Dutch are at times curious to understand my story and how I came to the point where I could speak Dutch fluently. The language also helped me to complete my studies and secure a good job as a student. Also, I would not have been able to work with the ambulance team and to meet Danny, who encouraged me and pushed me to pursue my education. Furthermore, I would not have been able to get my first job after my study. My confidence would not have grown. And I doubt I would still be there, and this could have a big impact on my ability to become who I am today.

The inability to speak, understand, and write the language of the community that you live opens up space for uncertainty, confusion, and fear, and could slow an individual's speed to success. By being able to interact with others in your community, you acquire more knowledge, know more people, and have better understanding of the culture of the people in that community and much more.

IT MAKES LIFE EASIER TO AN EXTENT

I remember during my first year of working with this particular hospital. Before they considered me as a foreign employee, the hospital needed to apply for a residence permit. It happened that I was the first case they had to handle, and they did not know how to go about it. This made getting my work permit longer to process, to the extent that I almost lost my job. Since I spoke Dutch, a co-worker invited me for lunch together with someone that worked at the city council, where the worker's permits are. I was able to express myself in the Dutch language, and this person helped me to facilitate the process. I was able to receive my work permit just one week after the incident. Just imagine what would have happened if I was unable to express myself in Dutch. My job would have been at stake. If I had allowed discouragement, self-doubt, and pity to take over me when I was learning the language, I wouldn't have gotten to this stage in life. At a certain point, you might not know what is down the lane, but keeping the faith will undoubtedly take you on an incredible journey.

DEALING WITH NEGATIVITY

Negative words and reactions from friends and

acquaintances are also some things you need to learn how to handle with caution. They will undoubtedly set in at one point or the other, but do not give in to them. Do not be discouraged by negative words and influence from a peer group. In life, everyone wants to get there first and fast, but in most cases, it is not everyone that finished first who will be most successful.

Also, pressure from family and friends will always be there, but if you can put them aside and stay focused, the result would be glorious. It might not be 100% good at the beginning, but as you accelerate, you get better, and you begin to see that you can make it to the end of the road.

Always make sure you find reasons to succeed, and hold them close to your heart. Positivity helps you to attract more value into your life. Avoiding a negative environment should also be one of your major priorities if you want to succeed beyond the average man. The adverse climate could shift your attention to irrelevant things and distractions. I remember people telling me to stop school, get married and make money.

Do not take the words of someone saying you CANNOT make it. The word CANNOT sounds negative and depressing, but it should be a stepping stone to greatness, and a pathway to success rather than a setback word.

Remember that in life, many great men and women today were once told they could not be what they are today. They failed several times before they attained greatness. The only thing they did differently was that they refused to give up. So, don't give up on your dreams. No matter how long it might take, there is light at the end of the tunnel.

Trying to be like others or looking at other people's achievements in life would make you more discouraged. You may not know how they got to the position they are in today. You may not know their stories and their challenges. They were also discouraged and doubted themselves at some point. When we look at people, and what they have achieved in life, we might think we are wasting our time. This thinking might bring stress and discouragement, depending on how you relate or process it. Keeping a positive mind helps you prevail beyond discouragement and self-doubt.

At the age of 19, I was discouraged because of the challenges I was going through in a foreign land. I was concerned about the fact that my friends were already graduates, and I was still struggling to learn a language. I was discouraged and doubted if I could make it to this point in life. However, I came to the understanding that everyone is not the same. Our route to success does not have the same distance, nor the same price. Focus your attention on the result you want to get, rather than on who is finishing before us. This is what made the difference in my life.

KEEPING FOCUS

Keeping focus is the keyword. It might not be easy, but it is a powerful key to success. It facilitates your ability to achieve your goals in life. Losing focus in life can come in different forms. As a young lady, they were times I lost focus, got distracted, and wanted an easy-going life. I know you have been there as well. That moment you are tempted to turn to the easiest route even when you are aware that they won't give you a long-lasting result. It might be difficult at times to stay focus, but it is possible to learn it.

"Discouragement and self-doubt are sure to set in, they are part of the process. But as I said earlier, they don't mean you have been DEFEATED."

CHAPTER 5:

UNDERSTANDING THE DIFFERENCE BETWEEN MONEY AND SUCCESS.

"Money can come without success, but success never come without money."

THE DIFFERENCE BETWEEN MONEY AND SUCCESS

Almost everyone wants to move to Europe, America or any western country with the purpose of getting a good job, education, reuniting with family, and many more. As a younger lady, your understanding of the difference between money and success is very important in your journey to financial freedom and fulfilment. While keeping in mind that money is important, we also have to understand positioning and priorities when it comes to achieving good success. So, the question is, which one should come first, money or success?

The pursuit of money at times can make you go the wrong way. Many big dreams have been cut down because of the inability to differentiate between money and success. Money can come without success, but success never comes without money. What do I mean by this? Let me share a brief story with you. When I first came to Europe, I had the opportunity to work for as many hours and days as I like. I could make a lot of money by doing that. I would be able to send enough money back to my friends and family in Africa 'to make them feel that I am abroad.' I want you to note the way I put my last phrase 'to make them feel that….' This means that if I do that, I am not actually being truthful to myself, because I will be creating a feeling and not revealing the reality of my situation. During my stay in Europe, I have noticed that one of the biggest challenges to success is the inability of most immigrants, especially those coming in from Africa, to make a differentiation between money and success.

More than 90% of Africans who travel abroad always have high expectations, and expect sudden financial breakthrough upon their arrival. However, when they finally arrive, the sudden realisation that dreams can only be translated into reality with massive action comes into place. This creates an enormous gap between what they want and the reality. This can come with a lot of depression, and sometimes, it can be traumatising. This may push some people to look for ways to get money by all means. Getting money by all means is what I call money without success.

Success comes with personal development and progressive growth. It comes with building a network of supporters. People who can stand by you and give you encouraging words when you are down. I can trace some of my biggest wins in my success journey to the network I built over the years. My first win was my elder sister. Just the fact that she invited me to live with her in Europe was actually my first step to success. I did not realise it at first, but whenever I sit and reflect, I am always grateful to God for making her think about me. In chapter two, I also wrote about Mr. Razman, and how he contributed to my success when I was taking the Dutch lessons. His support and the accountability approach he put in place for me helped me to always be among the top performing students in class. My participation in class also improved because of his encouragement and support. He would always ask me, "Did you do your assignment, and did you prepare well for the class?" Through his help, I became more focused, and I was able to complete my Dutch lesson, which helped me get started with my education and have my first job as a student. I took him as my 'big brother.' He looked out for me in school, and I could talk to him whenever I had any issues. As you move up your ladder of success, you will meet people like Mr. Razman that will also help you achieve success. This brings us to one of the keys to financial freedom and fulfilment, which is accountability. However, we will not be dealing with accountability in this chapter. We will talk more about it in chapter 10.

Building a System for Success

In addition, Rev. Father Chima was another person who played a major role in my success journey. He made me feel that he understood my challenges as a young lady. He supported me spiritually and psychologically as a priest. This is the kind of support we all need to succeed. He went an extra mile by introducing me to a nurse who understood my culture and beliefs better, and was in a better position to give me extra support. I remember one of the conversations I had with the nurse during lunch that really helped me build a stronger success culture. She made me to understand that becoming a nurse was a good choice. She also made me understand that there was diversity in nursing field. I could be a paediatric, general, social, psychiatric nurse and many more. Speaking to this lady marked one of the turning points in my life. I had the courage to overcome fear of the unknown. I also gained confidence and believed more in myself.

I also remember Hilda. She was responsible for the foreign students in the nursing school. She was there to support me socially, and was instrumental to my success in school. She helped me find a suitable student accommodation, and also helped me integrate myself in the community. She made me feel at home, introduced me to her family and took me along with her when she had family parties, birthday parties, and even Christmas dinners. She was an angel, a teacher and a friend. Whenever I did not understand any course, she made out time and explained everything to me in English, so that I would have a better understanding. The culture and lesson I learned from these incredible people along my journey to success is what brings me fulfilment today as a lady. I have been able to understand the value of sharing, and the importance of standing the gap and holding space for those who just need a little push to succeed in life. This is how easy success can be.

To the best of my understanding, success is not about how much you know, but how well you relate with the people that have the knowledge of what you need.

The other two great people I also met in my success journey were Kristal and Aquinas-Thomas. God has a way of bringing divine helpers my way when I really need them. This has been a continuous pattern in my life, and I have learned how to draw from my understanding of my previous success to have more success. The reason I am sharing these short stories with you is because I want to build your hope and encourage you to understand that in the journey of success, it is not about what you know, but your ability to situate yourself in a community of great people like Kristal and Aquinas-Thomas. These helpers became good friends of mine. Kristal was a nurse, and she graduated from the same school where I was studying. We first met during an event while I was working with the ambulance team. She was so nice to me. The first time we met, we talked a lot about school and personal life. She gave me her number and said to me, "Monica you can call me anytime you need help." After the event, I had an appointment to meet with her at her residence, and from there, the relationship grew stronger. She was of great support to me. Her mama would always make sure she cooked for us. Kristal would also help me go through an assignment or report.

Aquinas-Thomas, is also a friend. A Ghanaian, but he is so good with languages. He can speak, read and write Dutch as if he is a native speaker. I got to know him through Hilde, my lecturer. Hilde had previously told me that there was a man called Aquinas that will be coming from Ghana to study computer science in Dutch. A day after he arrived Turnhout, Hilde invited me for dinner so that I could meet him. I remembered after dinner, I noticed he was too nice. My first word to him was 'I have a boyfriend, so keep your distance (laughs).' That was just a side distraction. Aquinas-Thomas was of substantial support to my success journey. His computer abilities were outstanding. He would always help me out when my computer was bad, or when I had a problem with Microsoft word and language. When I felt like giving up, he was always there to encourage me. At times when the deadline to submit my report was just around the corner, he would always make sure he comes over and work with me until the report is done and submitted. This is one of the reasons why I said earlier on that you do not need to know everything in other to succeed, because you will always meet people like Aquinas-Thomas that will be an integral part of your success.

You might be thinking that you are alone in this journey. I used to think so too, but meeting these great people who helped me succeed, and made life easy for me gave me a new perception about success. Meeting Professor Chika Unigwe was another great encounter. Meeting her and learning about her success journey gave me more courage, and reasons why I should never quit in my drive for success. She had also travelled abroad at a very young age but could navigate through all the language barriers and emerge very successfully. In addition, when I meet her, she took me like her own sister and I became part of her family. Her circle of friends and the calibre of the people I had access to through her network was truly amazing. Her success story itself was a great lesson for me.

SEPARATING YOURSELF FROM FAILURE

No one has ever planned to fail. On the other hand, failure to plan strategically is the main reason many people do not have success. Unfortunately, majority of the people that are not succeeding are doing a lot to get out of their miserable situation. The only difference is that 'they are trying to eat peanuts from a transparent bottle without taking off the cap.' This is where mentorship and networking comes in to fill the gap. Let's look at the role of a mentor: A mentor is someone that has gone through a path that you are about to take, and is knowledgeable enough to caution you not to make the same mistakes that he/she made while pursuing the path. On the other hand, networks are communities of motivated individuals that are committed and motivated to share positive information that can enable you to advance your career.

In addition, there are also another set of people you will not like to miss on your way to success. They are called coaches. Coaches go beyond all odds to ensure that you succeed in whatever you do. They do this constantly, holding you accountable and pointing you to the right resources and directions for success. Coaches also play the role of mentors and are situated in networks that are very beneficial for your success. They are like the light you need when everything seems dark.

In my journey to success, coaching has played a key role in every step and it is also one of the key reasons you are reading this book right now.

MY SISTER, MY FIRST COACH

I must say, I am very thankful to have an elder sister like Mary. Sister Mary has been my coach. She has always paid attention to everything I do and is very good with follow-up, most especially throughout my life in Europe. When I moved to live with her and her family, she ensured I took all the necessary step I needed to meet my goals. When my resident permit was about to expire, she was restless, just to make sure I had all I needed to continue my legal stay in Europe. My sister and her husband, both being graduates, understood the importance of education, and supported me until I achieved success. They both supported me financially and emotionally. The support from the rest of my family was also outstanding. I am blessed to have six wonderful sisters and a brother. Thank you all for your support.

The great support I received from these beautiful people I have mentioned is to encourage you to know that you are not alone, and you will never be lonely in the pursuit of success. Most people that seek success also seek joy, and they will be thrilled to share and support you along with your endeavours. Most times, we become a stumbling block to our own success, simply because we fail to take action for the fear that we might not finish if we start. They are a lot of successful people that made it by faith. Faith and hope are your biggest strengths in life and you have to always take advantage of it to achieve more in life.

Thinking Beyond Your Comfort Zone

At any point in life, when you set your mind to understand that you can do more, you will always do more. When I started looking for other ways to add value to myself, I keep my mind open and I was willing to learn. I always looked forward to opportunities where I would be able to use my experience to help other young ladies going through similar challenges, as I did when I first arrive abroad. One afternoon, I was going through my Facebook page and I came across Dr. Francis Mbunya's video on starting a business at zero cost. I paused for a while and I said to myself, "How on earth can one possibly start a business at zero cost?" I took a step of curiosity and contacted him via Facebook, and we began a conversation. Initially, my idea of contacting him was to find out how he could help with a business idea we were already implementing, but was not working out well. However, during a conversation with Dr. Francis, he was able to point out some of my key strengths, which could be very valuable. After seeing my passion to help young ladies make a change in their livelihood, he advised me to write a book. I immediately told him it was not possible because I have never thought about that. I did not know how to start and what exactly to write. He said he will coach me, and that I am going to see how easy the process will can be and how it will add value to my life.

At the beginning of the coaching process, I was skeptical, not confident, had self-doubts and could not see the value he was seeing in me. After few coaching sections, things began to get clearer and clearer. Just before I knew it, I started writing in a flow. With his coaching process, I overcame self-doubt. I began to see that there is more to life and the possibility of you getting more is in your next step. I was surprised that it took me less than two weeks to write all my chapters and get the first draft of my book, which you are now reading. You can do the same, just by taking an action to get that dream home, husband, job or what so ever you desire. It starts by you understanding that you have the capability to do more. Set your mind today to win.

CHAPTER 6:

$\blacklozenge$────────$\bullet$────────$\blacklozenge$

EDUCATION IS PART OF YOUR SUCCESS

"The simplest way to do something you do not know is to learn it."

WHY DO YOU NEED FORMAL EDUCATION?

I agree with the general saying that academics is not for everybody. It is generally said that not all the great and wealthy men and women on earth went to school. This is true, but the question is whether the same situation will apply to you. Every individual on earth is different. You have to be able to identify your unique strengths in life. This will help you understand what works for you. Many people have gone astray in life today, because they think they can do the same thing that others do, and succeed the way they succeeded. This is definitely not true. This is because you do not have the same life they have.

I understood from the onset of my career that achieving better education was a plus for me to achieve success in life. I want you to understand that a good academic foundation is very important. It forms the basis of your success. It makes live easy for you and helps you to do more in less time. I understand most of the time that the process may seem very long and complicated. It was like that for me. However, there is always a starting point. The key is to focus on the good you can do today to be better tomorrow. I started with learning the Dutch language because that was the basis for me to achieve success. I understood that I couldn't do much without understanding the language of the country I am living in. I could still have some level of success without studying the language. I know a couple of people that have done that. However, there are only but one in a thousand people that have been able to go through that route and succeed. Based on my knowledge, I also know that they would have tripled their chances of success if they were able to speak the language of the country they found themselves in.

BRIDGING THE LANGUAGE BARRIER

In any part of the world you find yourself, language could be a barrier. When I talk about the language, I also look beyond the concept of reading and writing. Understanding the culture and norms of a people is also part of the language. For instance, in Belgium where I live today, there are specific cultures, seasons, celebrations and sayings that are peculiar to the people. You might not really understand the rationale or importance, until you situate yourself in understanding their language and history. I believe the majority of you reading this book can relate to this as well. Going back to the basis of language, which refers to reading and writing, I can say that understanding the Dutch language was a great stepping stone for me to gain admission into the nursing school in Belgium.

I can still remember the very first Dutch word I learned. I still laugh at myself today when I use the word. This is because, back then, I always hid behind the word to cover the fact that I did not understand the language well. The word 'JA', which simple means yes, was one of the first words I learnt in Dutch. Anytime someone asked me a question in Dutch and I did not understand, I would simply reply with, "Ja, ja, ja." This is because everyone I heard speaking the language also said those words. The second word I learnt faster was "shurgejonge jonge," which is an exclamation translated to, "O my gosh." I liked them because they were the most common words I could pick out of a conversation, and I could easily replicate them. Today, when I look back at those days, I simple shake my head and laugh at myself. This was the foundation that made me who I am today. Today I can speak Dutch fluently. I bet some beginners would even look at me and wonder if they could ever get to my level. I guess the answer is that you will might never learn how to walk if you are afraid to take the first step and fall. It's all about taking the first step without being afraid of failure. Anyone that have been in the venture of success will agree that at one point in time, they were not sure about the next day, but the next day came, and went past and they were still alive.

WALKING PAST THE FAILURE

In the previous chapter, I told you about the difficulties, discouragement, and challenges I went through while learning the Dutch language, and how Razman came to my rescue, right? That is exactly what happens when you refuse to bow to challenges and discouragement. God has a way of sending helpers your way when you set your mind to succeed above all odds. Razman noticed I was not doing well in class, and to him, he did not see the reason I should not succeed, given the potential he saw in me. I believe God used him to fast-forward me to my next level. His words and advice to me were healing and encouraging. I began to feel a strong need to not give up despite my fears and defeat. After my encounter with him, I realised that I magically started performing well in class without having to put in extra effort. You see, there are inner forces that aligns with our fears, and help to keep us on one spot. However, they are people that might definitely believe in you more than you believe in yourself. The fact that I was able to pursue another course beyond the Dutch lesson was also due to the confidence I had built in myself after Razman helped bring out some of my key strengths.

When I started studying another academic course (International Business management - IBMS), which was fully taught in English, I thought it would be easier because I had no major challenges expressing myself in English. However, I still noticed that it was still a major challenge to understand the lectures and meet the deadline for all my assignments. The entire course. was stressful and hectic for me. The reason I shared this is that I thought the major reason I was not doing well in the

Dutch lesson was because it was a foreign language. Yet, there I was in another program where I understood the language, but I was still facing the same challenges as in the Dutch lesson. This just goes to tell you that the major issue is not the language. It is more about the issue of the mind. The way our mind is structured toward a particular aspect of life puts a virtual barrier, which makes it difficult for us to move to the next level. In the Dutch class, the major reason I was having difficulty was because I had set my mind up to see the process as very difficult. In that case, no matter how easy the lecturer made it to be, my mind would not let me see it. What Razman simply did was to clear the block that was standing in my way and help me see the road more clearly. In the case of IBMS, my mind thought, it will be easier just because I knew it was taught in English. However, I did not take into full consideration my passion, my background and my future needs.

Seeing beyond any challenges requires our ability to see life in a three-dimensional view. This would help us differentiate our wants from our needs. Our minds easily go for what we are attracted to physically, rather than what we need. To align ourselves to the needs of our lives, we need to take a step beyond the physical sight. At the end of the day, my inner desire was not to study the IBMS.

I was simply attracted to the program because I thought it would be easy. When I revisited my desires and looked into my inner sight, I was able to see that nursing was my desire. The reason I was unable to see it by my physical sight was because I was more attracted to what my mind had decided would be easier.

GOING THE EXTRA MILE

At times, we might also need to travel an extra mile to meet the value of what will take us to the next step. This extra mile might still be at the beginning of our career, and we might not really see the need for it, but it is always important to communicate with our inner desires to align with what our soul actually needs to succeed. Discomfort and extra expenses might set in on our route of success. I remember I had to take extra Dutch classes in order to catch up with other students, and to stay on track with my assignment. This was definitely not comfortable at that time, but that was the extra mile I had to travel to enjoy the benefits today. When I also started my bachelor in Nursing, I had to spend long hours in the train just to ensure that I could attend my lectures in Belgium. I was still living with my sister in the Netherlands by then. Later on, I had to move to Belgium to look for a student accommodation and start living on my own. This was definitely not very comfortable compared to the type of good life I was used to in my sister house. However, this was another extra mile I had to travel in order to sacrifice for the future.

Sometimes, life demands that we have to do beyond our own capacity. Often, we give up with the excuse that we do not have what it takes, or with the excuse that we lack the resources needed to make the move. I could give all of these excuses then. I was very comfortable in my sister's house. Relocating was not the best option for me by then. However, I knew deep inside that I needed to take that step of faith to make it in life. While studying in Belgium, there were days and night I thought I would not survive till the next day, but God made a way in every situation that I went through. You see, there is no way God will put something in your heart, and not make a way for you to go through it successfully. The book of Jeremiah says that the thoughts God has for us are thoughts of good, and not of evil, to bring us to an expected end. My understanding and belief in this scripture has been a major foundation to my success because I know God is always walking with me in my hardest moments.

THE IMPORTANCE OF TAKING ACTION NOW

I saw the need to study, and prepare for my future while I was still young, and had less distractions. This is not to imply that you cannot achieve all of this while you are married. It is never too late to start, but an early start is a double advantage. You will also agree with me that when you start preparing for any activity well ahead of time, you set your mind at ease and free of worries. The secret of happiness is the joy of knowing ahead of time that you are on the winning side, despite the challenges that you might have on the way. What gives you strength in the midst of challenges is your mental preparedness to handle the challenge. Studying at an early age is easier than studying at a much older age. I believe one of the reasons I could easily handle the challenges that I had during my study as a young lady was because I had less distractions, and also because my mind was set for success.

My heart goes out to the young ladies because they have a huge advantage to take over their lives while the morning is still fresh. It is very easy for time to pass by, and we allow the distractions of life to distract us from the ultimate goal of financial freedom and fulfilment. Financial freedom and fulfilment for a young lady needs to be carefully planned and built into every step of their early life. The reason we have a lot of ladies going through some common challenges in life today, is because most of them are still trying to incorporate what they should have done several years back into the present period to find fulfilment.

Financial freedom and fulfilment do not come automatically in life. These are some issues we need to place a demand on in life. Anything of value has a price tag on it. The reason gold and diamond are very expensive is because of their value. The question I want you to ask yourself as a young lady reading this book is, "What value do I want to place on my life?" You have the opportunity to determine that value today. You have the opportunity to place any desire today, work hard towards it, and see it come to pass in less than no time.

You need to be able to prioritise between money and your academics. I also understand the challenges that many of us might be going through. The financial pressure from family members and friends who believe living abroad is a golden opportunity, and an easy way to make money. This is also one of the main reasons limiting many young ladies living abroad to attain financial freedom and fulfilment. They work too hard to satisfy their demanding family members, and friends from their country of origin. It is very important that you are able to support your family and friends. However, my advice for you is that you will be better placed to help them if you are able to invest in your value and capacity, most especially by focusing on achieving your academic goals.

CHAPTER 7:

DEALING WITH DAILY CHALLENGES

"Your secret to success is hidden in your daily routine."

EVERY DAY IS A WINNING DAY

In life, every day comes with its own challenges. How we choose to accept, handle and go about the daily challenges matter. Social relationships and emotional challenges in life could be well managed and converted to stepping stones. When they are properly managed, it helps us achieve more in life. Your ability to think well, and relate with your family, friends, loved ones and community is directly linked to how you manage the daily challenges that comes your way. On the other hand, when these challenges are mismanaged, it could cause delays, distractions, stress, frustration and even health challenges.

PUTTING ON A WINNING MINDSET

One of the things you have to do as a young lady wanting to succeed abroad is to put on a winning mindset daily. Many times, the society itself can fight our success. You might feel unwanted in some environments simply because people do not understand your value. This can be a very big issue to deal with, especially if you fail to be confident about yourself and tell yourself as many times as possible that you are made in the image of God, and not in the image of man. With this kind of mindset, you will be able to overcome daily challenges that arise as a result of segregation and human preferences. This is a very important issue to talk about because this is one of the common problems you will face as a young lady in your community, at school and even at your job.

One of the ways I have been able to handle this challenge is to surround myself with good people that understand human values, and are highly uplifting in their words and actions. I have already shared a lot about some of these incredible people that have been part of my success journey abroad in chapter five of this book. The fact that you have people like this who fully understand your values goes to explain that the main triggers of segregation is more individual than societal. In addition, you also need to fill your spirit with words of courage and prayers.

FINDING THE RIGHT ASSOCIATION

I remember my first school outing, I was twenty years old. That was my first school party. This party took place during my studies in The Netherlands. By then, I was studying International Business Management Studies (IBMS), so almost everyone who attended could understand the English Language because the program was taught in English. At the party, I could perceive that everyone was asking questions out of curiosity. I remember this girl walked up to me, and we were talking. She asked me if I would like a drink. I replied, no. She was surprised at my response, and even went further to ask, "Do you smoke?" I answered, "No, I have never smoked." She was still surprised at my response and asked further, "Do you have a boyfriend?" I replied, "No, I do not have a boyfriend." And then, she said, "Your life is so boring." She could not understand why I do not drink, smoke, nor have a boyfriend. This is because it was a common practice for a young lady at that age to either have a boyfriend, drink, or smoke. I was kind of lonely at that party because I could not fit in. It was not fun at all for me.

The above example is a typical example of wrong association. The reason I felt lonely at the party was because I could not identify with the habits of the other young ladies there. In that case, we could not speak the 'same language'. For me to feel accepted probably would have meant that I accepted the drink I was offered, and pretend to be like them. This is one of the major setbacks for many young ladies in today's society. This is where we have peer pressure setting in, and deviating many from their God given destiny. If I had accepted to belong to the larger crowd of the young ladies at the party, I cannot imagine what would have become of me today. At this time, you need time alone to have enough time in future to live a life of fulfilment.

Another thing to note here is that, you must be able to understand your cultural value and lifestyle while associating with the larger community. As a young lady coming from an African family filled with social values, everything I saw at the party was different from what I was taught to uphold as a young woman. Cultural difference is a very sensitive issue to deal with, and it must be handled with care because it has a very high potential to disrupt your lifestyle.

DEALING WITH EXCITEMENT

The excitement, luxury, freedom, and rights given to youths in the western part of the world is definitely not the same as for those of us coming from an African background. It is easy to get carried away by the things we come across while abroad. This might even make us to forget our primary purpose of traveling abroad. I know this does not apply to everyone. However, our awareness of our differences is very important, and will help us overcome many challenges and fast-forward our success journey.

I really did not enjoy my school days like most young persons my age did. I did not see this as a bad, but instead, as a price I had to pay in other to get a better future. In life, we must forgo some things in other to gain others. While my classmates were home relaxing after school, I had to go to work to raise extra money for myself, or attend Dutch lessons. I really did not have much friends because I did not have much time to hang out. I was either busy studying with my Dutch/English dictionary beside me, or I was out there cleaning, babysitting or working with the elderly to get some money into my pocket. I had to work every weekend in my third year in school, because during the day, I was either in school or at the hospital for placement. My inability to speak good Dutch also limited my potential to socialise. I did not have much confidence to communicate with people. This was also the reason why during my break periods, I'd rather go to the library, sit there in front of the PC, and browse through the internet while eating my lunch quietly. I was seen as anti-social, but they did not understand what I was going through. This did not bother me that much, though I envied other young ladies when I saw their families helping them out with lots of daily activities. However, this was one of the reasons I needed to work harder. I learned to turn the challenges around my daily schedule into my strength.

CULTURE AND FOOD

New foods, lifestyles, dressings, and behaviours can be hard to accommodate, and can alter your strength to win daily. Most of the time, I was discouraged to go out for lunch because I was not used to the food. Even when I pushed myself to go out for lunch because of hunger, making a choice from the menu list was always a big issue. Apart from the fact that I was struggling to understand the language, I did not understand the food combinations all together, because it was not what I was used to. To avoid disgracing myself most of the time, I would prefer not to go for lunch. However, this was not such a big issue because I still had the opportunity of enjoying my home-made Nigerian food occasionally.

CULTURE AND RELATIONSHIP

The dynamics and values of relationships varies across different cultures. A typical African, or someone from my native country, Nigeria, will understand that a valuable relationship is built around family, honesty, mutual respect, and sincerity. However, I am also aware this has shifted to a whole different phase in the last decade. We constantly witness cases where people no longer go into a relationship because of genuine love, and sincerity, but because they want to take advantage of their partner and so on. This kind of scenario might likely happen to a young lady who travels abroad and is not conscious of the differences in lifestyles and values. Moreover, for young ladies that want to make it the easy way in life, they often think that getting into a relationship for financial ego, and companionship is a way to go. Alternatively, this is one of the major sources of stress, and it delays your desire to attain success. There is definitely nothing bad in getting into a relationship. The major problem is the value and motives behind the relationship.

In a nutshell, I want you to understand that relationships could create emotional stress. Social pressure and responsibilities that accompanies a relationship needs to be well considered by both parties before they make the decision to proceed. At the time, when you are in a hurry to get into a relationship, it just gets your life more complicated than before, and because of that, you might also be in a hurry to get out.

CHAPTER 8:

DISCIPLINE, LIFESTYLE, AND HABITS

"The most useful weapon in the battle of success is discipline."

THE ACT OF BEING DISCIPLINED

Discipline will be your biggest tool to attaining success in whatever you do. Your ability to start and finish any task without distraction is determined by how disciplined you are. I know we are all familiar with word discipline, and we all wish we could be disciplined in one or most aspects of our lives. The question is, how do we achieve discipline in life? Or simply put, how can we set goals and easily achieve them? This brings us to talk about two types of discipline essential in our journey to success, and most importantly, in the life of a young lady. This might also apply to young men, but the reason I am peculiar to young ladies is because I am sharing my experiences as a young lady, and also because I have special attraction to seeing young ladies become successful.

SELF-DISCIPLINE

Self-discipline is a higher dimension of discipline attributed to leaders. When I talk about a leader, I mean anyone who masters what they should focus on. Leadership is more of an internal attribute than a physical attribute. Leadership starts with yourself. The ability to set goals and accomplish them with minimum external guidance, is the discipline required by young ladies to succeed in life. You need to be able to take control of your own life, and your own affair. You must have read the parts where I shared the things I did to prevail in times of challenges. That is an example of discipline, which is also attributed to leadership. You will also notice that in most of the cases where I overcame the challenges, I had to lean on the shoulders of someone else. This is just to say that no matter how discipline you might be from the inside, you still need external support to succeed. The reason self-discipline is a principal tool for success is because it prompts you to take actions without waiting for external motivation. You need to be self-started.

EXTERNAL DISCIPLINE

External discipline is from the outside. This is the discipline that is needed by anyone struggling through a challenge. You can achieve this by surrounding yourself with a group of uplifting and motivated people that are more effective than you are in specific areas. This is also easily achieved by having a mentor or a coach that can commit to your success, and hold you accountable for your actions. Although coaching and mentorship used to be reserved for the professional or educational career, it is fast gaining ground in social life. We could easily meet our daily goals by leveraging the power in coaching or mentorship.

Being disciplined can help you achieve your goals faster. The reason we struggle to do a lot most of the time is because we are not disciplined enough to find out what we should be focusing on. Blueprints are taking over the world now. We have gone past the time when distance was a barrier to learning, or when people needed to meet face-to-face in order to learn. With social media and other related facilities, it has become easy to reach the world in just one click. However, we need to be disciplined and learn how to use it for good. It is also worthy to note that, despite the advantages of the social media in terms of facilitating global connection and getting work done easily, it is also the major form of distraction. This is why discipline is a very important aspect in today's economy where almost everything has gone online.

HUMILITY AND DISCIPLINE

One of the key features of discipline is humility. My friend, Kristel, taught me a lot, and helped review my reports which I was in school. I believe the reason she did that was because I was humble enough to admit I needed extra help, and I needed to learn from her. These are services I would have paid for if I had chosen not to learn humility and discipline. There are many people you will meet on your way that will have the ability, or the potential to help you. However, whether they help you or not depends on how humble you are to ask for that help.

Instead of trying to do everything all by yourself, which is still okay and possible, it is always a double advantage to have external help. In addition, having a trustworthy person to account to, also helps you stay focused and discipline. Just the fact that you are accountable to someone else is a great sense of discipline.

When you are focused and disciplined, you can easily achieve your goals. This helps you keep moving ahead, and add more value to your life. Most great men and women that are successful will always tell you discipline and focus have been a great source of strength.

LIFESTYLE

It is very important for you to take good care of your health. A healthy lifestyle will fast forward your winnings. Feeling discouraged, not eating well and healthy, not having enough sleep, and over thinking are all detrimental to your success. These may trigger stress, and if care is not taken, it could lead to depression, stomach ulcer, stress ulcer, continuous headache, and heart problems. Besides this, peer group pressure, and pressure from family can push you to set unrealistic goals in order to meet up to their expectations. Most of these things happen in our lives, and we might not be conscious of the fact that it is because of the kind of lifestyle that we are living. I remember being a victim of stomach ulcer during the period of my studies. I took all types of medication in order to eradicate it, but it did not get better. At one point, I had to stop all the medications and start eating all the food I was restricted from eating as a result of the ulcer. I stepped up my faith in prayer and improved my lifestyle by eating healthy, eating on time, and worrying less. Just by doing this, I did not have to be on any medication any longer.

Some causes of poor lifestyle and stress can be linked to poor planning and preparation. Most especially when you are studying and preparing for exams. Students in particular are known to become addicted to energy drinks and coffee during an examination period. This subjects the body to unusual behaviour, which the system might not be able to accommodate due to the rapid changes in lifestyle. I was also a victim of this. Coffee and energy drinks almost caused me to develop a heart problem. I remember during one of the examination periods, I had to rely on energy drinks on a regular basis to stay awake and study for a longer period. A day came when I could no longer breathe well because of the overdose. I started feeling a high pressure in my chest. I was very uncomfortable and could not study well again. This caused me to perform very poor in the exam. I had to sleep for longer hours in order to regain myself. The time I was trying to gain, was all gone.

It is very important to eat well, sleep well, drink a lot of water, and avoid energy drinks and coffee when possible. If possible, make out time to travel. I know making time for travel might not always be feasible given the tight schedule and limited resources, but it is one of the most powerful mind healers. Taking out weekends to visit family, friends, or attend social functions is also a good way to practice living a healthy lifestyle. In my case, I had the opportunity and the means to travel once in a while. Traveling is also an important activity, most especially for people that are working, as it helps to free the mind and create more space for creative thinking. Setting time for traveling will help you overshoot your goals and increase your productivity.

CREATING HOBBIES THAT WORK FOR YOU

It is also important to pick out hobbies that will help you relax and distract yourself from too much stress and burnouts. For instance, I love listening to music because it makes me happy. At times, I will find myself unconsciously dancing to it. Picking a hobby that elevates your feelings, and makes you happy is a good medication for your health. One of the strategies I adopted to avoid wrong association and influence from peer pressure, was to find and do the things that kept me motivated and happy out of my study time.

HABITS

Although healthy habits may be understood differently by different individuals, it forms the foundation of successful people. Your habit is a reflection of your daily routine. The time to wake up from bed, go to sleep, what you eat, your spiritual life, the type of people you associate yourself with, and so on are the things that define you as a person and also affects the way you live.

I have been able to adopt some of these healthy habits that have contributed to my growth and success in life. One of them which is very close to my heart is cultivating a healthy prayer and spiritual life. Praying, and being a spiritual lady has helped me to discern and overcome many challenges that I would normally not be able to overcome with a non-spiritual mindset. It has also built me to worry less and trust more in God in all my ways. In addition, I also make sure to exercise regularly, eat healthy whenever possible, travel at the least opportunity and surround myself with positive minded friends. I cannot overemphasize the role of healthy habits in the journey to success. Although this is sometimes under-looked, it is a powerful success tool.

CHAPTER 9:

PERSISTENCE

"Persistence is the fuel needed to drive success."

PERSISTENCE IS THE KEY WORD

Persistence, what a sweet word to pronounce, but not too easy to keep up with. It takes the grace of God, courage, sound mind, focus, and good advice to keep persisting till you reach your goal. It sounds easy when people say, "Keep pushing. C'mon, others are doing it, so can you." It is true that you are smart and intelligent, but they will only be revealed when you prevail through daily challenges as discussed in chapter 7.

One of the biggest lessons I have learnt during my success journey is that persistence comes with relentless action. I also learnt that, you do not need to know what will be the final result before taking a positive action. Your actions should be based on a sound judgement of right or wrong, valuable or not valuable, useful or not useful, relevant or not relevant. These are some standard words that have guided me in taking positive steps every day, that have all together contributed to who I am today. You also have to be aware that there is a great invisible system of support available when you set out to add value for yourself. You will always meet people along the way who definitely want you to succeed. I also met such people along my journey to success, and I am still meeting them today. This is an indication that these types of people are always available. You might have had some bad experiences meeting some certain people along your way, but that does not mean that everyone is the same. Persistence is what keeps you on track, and also directs you to encounter people of value.

When I started my Dutch lesson, I was discouraged and I almost gave up. I often had to drag myself to the class with little or no zeal to learn. When I kept persisting, it paid off. I crossed paths with Razman who saw my persistence despite my lack of zeal. He encouraged me, and that was the beginning of success for me. When you persist, you will definitely find strength and courage to move the next level.

LISTENING TO THE LITTLE VOICE WITHIN

At times, the voice outside is louder than the voice inside. This might be a major stumbling block to your journey to success. I remember while studying for my bachelor degree in nursing, my teacher told me I was not fit enough to be in the program. She advised that I withdraw, and instead study a diploma in nursing. Although I was going through some challenges at that moment, which was affecting my performance, that did not mean that I was not fit for the bachelor program. The external voice judges based on what it sees, but the internal voice is the conviction within you. You will agree with me that if you are not internally convicted, you will not take the first action. The first actions are most often what your mind desires. The check has to be whether what the mind desires is right or wrong. When it is right, then you need to apply persistence to prevail through the process. The fact that I did not listen to the voice of my teacher was because I knew within me that I was up to the task. Do not let people that do not understand what you are going through talk you out of your destiny.

I was also told that I could not specialise as an intensive and emergency care nurse. I could have just agreed with what they were thinking about me, and agree with their opinion. However, I knew I was not born to settle for less. I knew that there was a word called persistence. I was able to look at my past victories, and draw strength from there. I thought about what happened during my Dutch lesson, and how I finally made it through. Your ability to persist is a conscious act. You need to be able to look at some of your past victories and draw inspiration from them. You also need to feed yourself with positive affirmations, so that what you have inside of you could control what is outside of you. For me, I found strength in praying and studying the bible daily. This has been a powerful tool that has helped me, and is still helping me win all battles in life. The reason we need to persist in every good venture we are in is because the world is not designed to make things easy for us. The word persistence itself exists because you need it to succeed in life.

However, one of the roles of persistence is that the gain at the end of the road needs to be greater than the pain. This is what give you the courage to persist. During my study, I persisted because I could see my bachelor degree certificate just around the corner. The thought and feeling of it being in my hands made me not give up. My being persistent definitely has yielded fruits beyond my degree. Many other doors have been opened to me because of my ability to persist. Working today as an intensive and emergency care nurse in one of the prestigious university teaching hospitals in the world is not a small feat. In writing this book, there were times I felt discouraged and wanted to turn to an easier option. It is obvious that the easier option is to give an excuse, and not do it or push it to another time. Applying the concept of persistence was easier here because I was surrounded by positive energy, and continuous encouragement from my coach. I would like to emphasize here that persistence is sponsored by positive energy. You need to constantly find motivation and stronger reasons not to quit. In today's world with a lot of distractions from the outside, including friends that do not want to take responsibility for their lives, having a coach or a mentor is definitely the best winning strategy you can think of, if you dare to succeed beyond the normal society norms. To separate yourself from ordinary happenings, you need to connect to go the extra mile.

LEVERAGING GOODWILL FOR PERSISTENCE

The help I received from some family members, friends, and people of goodwill whom I met along my career path is an indication of the resources available to anyone who wants to take action, and take charge of their life. There is a lot of support available for anyone who wants to rise above their current situation. What you need to do to access it is to first, come to the realisation that this help is available. This gives you the courage to step out of your fear. I know at times it is difficult to know exactly where to start off with. My advice for you is that the best place to begin is within your own community, and more specifically, in the church. I have been able to find a lot of help and encouragement daily, by fellowshipping in my church. The church is always a great place to start because you have a lot of people who can uplift your spirit, pray with you when you need encouragement, and support you in time of need. I can't count the number of times I have had to call my pastor, and he would just pray with me and give me encouraging words when I need extra strength to persist. They always go the extra mile to make sure I am doing okay. The church is definitely my second home because the environment is so lovely and safe.

DISTRESS IS RELEVANT FOR GROWTH

I also remember that when I started my bachelor's degree, I travelled every day from The Netherlands to Belgium to attend classes. I had to spend several hours between the train and the bus just to go to, and from school. This went on until I finally found a suitable student accommodation in Belgium. The distress was relevant for the success I have achieved today. Getting accommodation was also a process of distress and persistence. I remembered being rejected by some owners of student accommodation for reasons I could not really justify. I was frustrated, but did not give up. I had to persist and find extra help, and ways to go around the rejection. I was opportune to meet one of the administrators in my school, called Hilda. She was so friendly, and helped me get accommodation with ease because of her influence. If I had allowed rejection to stop me from moving ahead, I would not have gotten the accommodation. I also encountered many obstacles on the way that would have made me give up. One of the incidents I encountered was the period when I had to register for swimming classes. When I went to register for a lesson, I was rejected simply because I could not speak Dutch fluently. I persisted, and did not give despite the rejection. As in the case of the accommodation, I had to still find a way to enrol because I knew the benefits of the lesson. I spoke to one of my teachers in school, and she was able to intervene. I was finally accepted into the class.

The spirit of persistence helps you to press on until you get what you want. It does not give room for quitting, and it is not for losers. Most great men and women, billionaires and millionaires in the world today would tell you that they did not give up. When they failed, they stood up. Though at times, it was very difficult, but they kept rising and pressing until they achieved their dreams.

I know it was difficult for me. The challenges were sometimes unbearable, heavy, annoying, frustrating, embarrassing, and discouraging, but I did not give up because I knew what I wanted. I had the dream to become a nurse, and every time I felt like quitting, I compared the pain of not making it to the gain of seeing my dreams come true. I also remembered the expectations from my family and friends, and the efforts of all the people of goodwill that were there for me. All of these gave me the courage and strength to keep pressing on to achieve my goals.

PERSISTENCE IS A COMPANION IN LIFE

Persistence is a companion in life. It helps you not to give up until you get to the finished line. The major drive that helped me to persist and prevail through the hard moments was to focus on the end results. The focus on the end results helps you to overlook distractions that might be on the way. Let's say you need to drive every day to work, and your route cuts across a major city. Just because there is a traffic jam on the way on some days would not stop you from going to your job, right? It might take you a longer time than normal to arrive. However, you will still get to work, because that is your ultimate goal. Sometimes you might even reroute in other to still get to the same destination. The ability not to give up while in the traffic jam on your way to work, or to school is what I call persistence.

I did not allow the speed of the others who seem to be moving faster than me in life distract me. I knew for one reason, or the other, we were not in the same lane of life and that is definitely the truth. I clearly understand that relocating to another country, mostly from Africa to western countries in order to seek for a better livelihood, comes with a lot of pressure and expectations from family and friends. This comes because of the sacrifices they might have committed into your traveling. Most often, this becomes a major distraction in our journey to success, because the high expectations put pressure on us to want to over commit to meeting our goals. This will lead to stress and burnout, which are the major causes of failure.

It is of important that we understand the goal and foundation of success. There is no building that will stand strong without a solid foundation. Quite often, the pursuit of success throws us off the lane, and instead of persisting on the right part, we focus on pursuing money rather than success. We have previously discussed the difference between success and money. At times when we miss our priority, we find out that the strength to press on fails. It is also very important that we do not allow the achievement of others to affect us negatively. Instead, it should encourage us to know that, if they could make it, we can also make it. Adding value to your life is all about going after what is valuable.

CHAPTER 10:

◆━━━●━━━━━━━━━━━●━━━◆

CAN I REALLY MAKE IT AS A YOUNG LADY IN A FOREIGN COUNTRY?

"You started writing your story the day you made up your mind."

ASKING THE RIGHT QUESTIONS

They were thousands of questions that ran through my mind when I first arrived in the Netherlands some years back. As a young lady full of aspirations, I was confronted with a lot of challenging questions. I had to deal with the language issues, financial issues, academic issues, health issues and many more. This was normally not beyond my expectations. I was expecting to see everything go very easy. You might find yourself at that same point in life now, where you are asking yourself a lot of questions. At times you might even think that you made the wrong choice. The good news is that you did not make a wrong choice. The problem is that there is actually no problem. You are just seeing the problem from a different lens, that is why it seems difficult to fix. Immediately you come to the understanding that the problem can be solved, you will be 90% close to the solution.

All these questions and many more that runs through your mind are normal. The experiences you are going through are steps on your way to success that make you stronger and steadfast. In other words, they are merely distractions to make you lose focus on your final destination. The solution starts by your ability to understand the new system, and the environment you currently find yourself in. if you did follow me well in the previous chapters of this book, I cited several occasions I almost gave up, but finally found strength. You will also notice that in most of my narrations, the help I found was already available even before I started looking for it. In the Dutch class, I was there all the time with Razman, but never knew he was a great resource until we crossed paths one day. The reason you are also reading this book today is because there is help available for you, no matter what challenge you might be going through.

Most of the challenges in life are virtual. This means that they don't really exist beyond our thinking until we give them the permission to become a reality. Have you ever thought about a particular food you dislike? What happens when the thought of that food comes to your mind? You immediately dismiss the thought, right? This is because you do not want your mind to dwell on it. Immediately you dismiss the thought, you automatically replace it with something else you prefer. Let's look at it from another direction. What if a thought about your favourite food comes to your mind? You will want to go an extra mile to have it because you've allowed your mind to dwell on the thought.

This is exactly the way life happens. Unfortunately, unlike the thought of the food we dislike, we instead turn to allow the thoughts of our challenges dwell in our mind. What makes a thought to be established is the amount of attention we give to it. This is also the reason why persistence is one of the keys to a winning strategy. It allows your mind to dwell on the activity in question long enough for the solution to surface on its own. While I was studying, I was told several times by some of my teachers that I should quit and do something else. I did not quit because I couldn't get my mind off the fact that I wanted to become an intensive care nurse. In addition, my persistence also brought the results I needed to emerge victorious.

OVERCOMING SUCCESS BLOCKAGES

I am aware that we all need money to live a sweet life. I am also aware that money is a big blockage to financial freedom. The pursuit of money can be the reason you do not also get the money you need. For you to be able to handle any financial need beyond the basic needs of life, you need to bypass the pursuit of money and start pursuing success. We discussed the difference between success and money in chapter five. As a young lady, you have to be very wise in setting your priorities. There is the general conception that young African ladies who travel to the western countries only come to make money, and not to achieve success. One thing about the pursuit of money is that it will never lead you to fulfilment. Fulfilment is more about a sense of belonging and acceptance that only happens within the individual. The reason you might have many unhappy rich people is because they lack fulfilment.

Discouragement is also a major roadblock to financial freedom and fulfilment. At times, we might feel depressed, lost, and confused. These are feelings that come to distract us. We always have to try not to stay in there for a long time. Staying out of depression and confusion is a big win in life. This might seem challenging. That is why you always need to leverage the help of people around you who have experience handling a similar situation. These often are people that have gone through the challenges and have successfully overcome them.

Another important road block to watch out for as a young lady is rejection. Do not allow rejection to make you feel less important, or like an outcast. These are attitudes you will surely come across. However, try not to let it sink into you. I had some of my fellow African classmates who gave up on their nursing career because of rejection and challenges. I wish they understood that it was all temporal. I was able to prevail because I understood that the gain at the end was more that the pain of enduring through the rejection. By the grace of God, I was able to stay strong and keep calm till I got what I wanted. I definitely knew it was a trial and a phase that will pass.

Stay focused, disciplined, and keep pressing on. Know that you CAN DO it. You can become that great lady in life, you can add value to your life. You will be able to better assist your family and community if you are able to overlook the pursuit of money and focus on the pursuit of success. This means that you need to be able to fight all the challenges that comes along in the school of greatness. Life could be much easier if you can manage your worries in the right way. I want you to imagine what life will be and how you will feel if you were able to assist your family with less stress. I want you to imagine what impact you can have in your community if you could achieve your goals and start living a good life.

It is never too late to start dreaming again. Whenever you want to take action and get back on track to pursue your goals, always know that you have equal chances to succeed as someone who started a couple years before you. It is possible to realise your dreams in no time. Do not allow discouragement and self-doubt make you think you cannot achieve your goals. Have the faith and belief that there are always processes and systems that could help you move faster in life. Learning from someone that has been there is a big plus. Do not allow people's achievement to discourage you. However, look at the positive end of it, and learn from it. Most importantly, avoid negative energy, associations, and people without vision.

It is important that you take good care of your health and practice a healthy lifestyle. Keep pressing on until your gaols are fully achieved. Persistence will surely make room for success, and create wider doors for opportunities to flow in. Focus on your past successes to attract more success. In addition, discipline is a key attribute for success. It helps you to stay focused. It could be difficult to sustain persistency at the time, but do not lose hope. Be on the lookout for accountability partners and coaches that could hold your hand, and hold space for you to succeed in life.

The role of a coach is an ultimate solution to your success for two major reasons. The first is that they have passed through the express, so they are well equipped to handle the situation. Secondly, they operate in a network of successful and influential people. They have the ability to introduce you to people of value that could play a key role in your journey to financial freedom and fulfilment. At this point, I will still like you to take a moment and reflect on your values as a young lady by answering these questions we earlier discussed in chapter three.

- What is stopping you from achieving the life you want?

- What is stopping you from having a well-paid job?
- What is stopping you from writing that book?
- What is stopping you from starting that business?
- What is stopping you from getting married?
- What is stopping you from having a peaceful home?

These are all questions that if not carefully answered, will slow down your journey to financial freedom and fulfilment. Now that you have been able to learn the strategies that can help you achieve financial freedom and fulfilment, what action have you put in place to make sure that you acquire the success you deserve? Based on my experience, the best way to make sure that you stay on top of your goals is to work with an accountability coach. This does not mean that you cannot do it on your own. The difference is in the chances of success that come with working with an accountability coach and implementing it on your own. Statistics have shown that those with accountability coaches have an 80% chance to succeed in anything they do, while those without accountability coaches have 20% chance of success. My wish for you is that you are able to get to the faster lane of success by taking an extra step today, and investing in an accountability coach because they won't stop at nothing until they make sure you hit your goals. It does not necessarily need to be me. I have invested in an accountability coach, and the results have been mind-blowing. The reason I was able to write this book in less than two weeks was because I worked with an accountability coach. You can do the same today and experience the results yourself.

CHAPTER 11:

CONCLUSION

"The only reason you will fail is if you don't take any action."

WHY I WROTE THIS BOOK

Working as a specialised nurse has not only been fulfilling to me as a young lady, but has also been able to provide me and my family with the financial freedom we need to stay focused, and on top of our goals without any major distractions. I have come to the understanding that fulfilment is being happy about where you are in life, and having the hope to do more because your current circumstances provide the means for a brighter future. Fulfilment for me also goes beyond self-actualisation, and places you in a position where you become a source of inspiration for the younger generation. One of the reasons I wrote this book is to inspire young ladies that earnestly seek genuine success. I write to send you words of encouragement and to assure that financial freedom and fulfilment is available for any lady that is willing to persist beyond the normal daily challenges. Most often, what the heart desires might not necessarily be what will lead us to success. The heart desires comfort and rest. Most young ladies turn to seek comfort and rest in the hands of wealthy men without necessarily considering their own need for success. This might seem to be an easy way to comfort, but I will assure that it is short-lived.

I have had other women of colour asked me on several occasions what I did exactly to be able to thrive in a foreign land and be at a position many think is unattainable. I would like to say that impossibilities are only constructed in the mind. There is no chance of failure for anyone who sets out their heart for success, and does what it takes without giving up. The challenges that are on the road to success are obvious challenges. I wrote this book to share my wins and challenges with you. Despite the challenges, the end result is always a big win.

SIX STEPS TO FINANCIAL FREEDOM AND FULFILMENT

Six steps to financial freedom and fulfilment will help you understand how to deal with the roadblocks that might be on your road to success, so that you can focus on the things that matter the most in your journey. The book starts by walking you through stages you might experience at the beginning of your journey, and how they can potentially affect your results along the way. In the second chapter, I share some personal experiences of how I have been able to leverage my understanding of daily challenges to prevail beyond the challenge.

The subsequent chapters discussed the step-by-step challenges you may encounter while on your walk to financial freedom and fulfilment. In chapter four, we discuss strategies you could implement to avoid discouragement. We laid emphasis on the fact that the way the society and our own community are built can sometimes unconsciously promote, discourage, and make us feel that it is difficult to succeed. We share how you could convert discouraging circumstances into winning stories, rather than letting the situation kick us back. In chapter five, we discussed the pursuit of money, how it could deviate from your journey to financial freedom and self-fulfilment. We did emphasise that big dreams could be ruined if you fail to understand the difference between money and success. In chapter six, we discussed the power of education in success. While acknowledging that education does not necessarily mean a higher qualification in academics, we dwelt on the fact that every individual should be able to understand their special needs and strengths, and to leverage this for their advantage. In chapter seven, we discussed how you could handle daily challenges that come along your walk to success. In life, every single day comes with its own challenges. How we choose to accept, handle, and go about these challenges matter a lot. Social relationships and emotional challenges could be well managed and converted to stepping stones.

In chapter eight, we moved ahead to talk about discipline, lifestyle, and habits. We did emphasize that discipline will be your biggest strength to succeed in whatsoever you do. Your ability to start and finish any task without distraction is determined by how disciplined you are. Healthy habits form the foundation of successful people. Discipline is an integral aspect of your lifestyle and plays a key role in having a healthy lifestyle, and healthy habits. In chapter nine, we discussed persistence. Persistence comes with relentless action. When you are able to prevail to the end of the road, you emerge a winner. My wish for you is that you win in life, and become very successful.

ACKNOWLEDGEMENTS

Special thanks to Almighty God the father, the Son, and the Holy Spirit for grace, mercy and strength to write this book.

I want to thank my beloved husband, Ogechukwu Achugamonye, for always standing by me, and for his support in writing this book.

To my elder sister, Adaobi Mary Okey Obineke. Her husband and children, who brought me over to the Netherlands and gave me such a great opportunity to become whom God created me to become. Thank you so much.

To my parents, siblings, and all those who helped, and supported me through my academic career and life journey in general. I say thank you.

I cannot forget to thank my coach, Dr. Francis N. Mbunya, for his motivation and inspiration that led to the realisation of this book. Thank you for helping me see what I could do beyond my nursing career. Thank you for helping me add more value to my life.

THANK YOU FOR READING

Thank you for reading my book. As an appreciation to all my female readers, and particularly young ladies earnestly seeking for good success, I would like to offer you a free one-hour conversation with me. Together, we will explore possible ways that will help you to achieve financial freedom and fulfilment as a lady. All you need to do is send me an email using my details below with the subject, "I am interested in learning more about financial freedom and fulfilment as a young lady.", and I will get back to you at my soonest.

You can also stay connected with me through social media, and you will be able to get more tips on how you can effortlessly make it through life as a young lady.

Email: monicme19@yahoo.com

Facebook: https://www.facebook.com/monic.oranugo

ABOUT THE AUTHOR

Monica Nwabugo Oranugo is an Intensive Care and Emergency Nurse at the UZ Leuven Campus Gaithersburg, Belgium. Born in Warri, Delta State in Nigeria, she was privileged to migrate to Europe in 2003 where she studied and got her degree and specialization. Monica got her bachelor degree in Nursing from Katholic Hogeschool Kempen Turnhout (presently called Thomas More Campus, Turnhout) in 2009. After working as an emergency nurse in AZ Turnhout for a couple of years, she went ahead to further her study, and became an Intensive Care and Emergency Nurse, at UC Leuven, Limburg, in 2014.

The journey to success for Monica as an international student, and currently as a professional has been filled with challenges, but still remains inspiring and educative at the same time. Her heart goes out to everyone who might be trapped on his/her way to success. She has a soft spot for young ladies because of some challenges she went through as a young lady seeking success in a foreign land. She wrote this book to share some of her experiences; the challenges, and how she converted them into success stories. Her goal is to see every young lady victorious in life.

Monica Nwabugo Oranugo is happily married, and lives in Belgium with her husband. She speaks English, Dutch, and Igbo fluently.

Printed in Great Britain
by Amazon